IMAGES
of Aviation

BOEING

William E. Boeing frequently sailed the sheltered inland waters of the Pacific Northwest aboard his beloved yacht *Taconite*. On September 28, 1956, the crew docked at the Seattle Yacht Club in a state of alarm. Boeing, just days shy of his 75th birthday, was declared dead on arrival—the victim of an apparent heart attack. In accordance with his wishes, the remains were cremated, and the ashes were scattered in pristine Canadian coastal waters, where he loved to cruise, relax, and fish for salmon. The Boeing Company separately operates a yacht called *Daedalus* for business entertainment. (Courtesy of the Boeing Historical Archives.)

ON THE COVER: Boeing pilots Richard "Dick" Taylor (left) and Jack Funk are working on bomb-tossing tests at Wichita. Taylor (1921–2015) was a World War II pilot who was later director of engineering during Model 737 development. Some historians consider the B-47 Stratojet to be the most important Boeing design because it was the first to incorporate the innovations of pod-mounted jet engines hung beneath a swept wing. This configuration is the hallmark of the many thousands of Boeing jets that followed. According to a news item from February 8, 1949, "The Model 450-3-3 (XB-47) jet bomber sets a transcontinental speed record from Larson AFB to Andrews AFB, Maryland covering 2,289 miles in 3 hours and 46 minutes." The B-47 went on to establish other records for speed over distance. (Courtesy of the Boeing Historical Archives.)

IMAGES
of Aviation

BOEING

John Fredrickson

ARCADIA
PUBLISHING

Published by Arcadia Publishing
Charleston, South Carolina

Printed in the United States of America

Library of Congress Control Number: 2016903346

For all general information, please contact Arcadia Publishing:
Telephone 843-853-2070
Fax 843-853-0044
E-mail sales@arcadiapublishing.com
For customer service and orders:
Toll-Free 1-888-313-2665

Visit us on the Internet at www.arcadiapublishing.com

This book is dedicated to the managers who most favorably influenced my 36 years at Boeing: Norman E. Jepsky (flight test), Stewart S. Berry (international traffic), Richard G. Miller (finance operations), and Allyn J. Murphy (employee services). They demonstrated vision, compassion, drive, social savvy, intelligence, and competence, all of which are expected at Boeing. They delivered the infrastructure necessary for the brilliant engineers, dedicated assembly mechanics, and other technical geniuses to create and deliver amazing products.

CONTENTS

ACKNOWLEDGMENTS

The generous assistance and cooperation of Michael Lombardi and Thomas Lubbesmeyer of the Boeing Historical Archives in Bellevue, Washington, was invaluable to the creation of this book. Our focus is on William E. Boeing, the company he founded, and a sampling of its products. The book offers a traditional (i.e., pre-merger) view of Boeing operations and products.

The designations for airplanes can be confusing. Boeing products are assigned a model number for internal purposes. Designs intended for military use are given a separate identifier by the owning service. Up until the late 1950s, the Navy and Air Force applied inconsistent designations to the same product. For example, Model 314 (Pan American Clipper) became the C-98 when commandeered by the Army (five airframes), while the Navy called it B-314 (four airframes).

Airlines generally observe the Boeing model designation. Model 747-100 was the world's first jumbo jet in 1970. Digits after the model number represent major design improvements, as when the 747-400 was superseded by the 747-8, which first flew in 2010. Freighters are airplanes with oversized cargo doors, no passenger seats, and sometimes no fuselage windows (e.g., 747F).

Narratives labeled as a "news item" were taken verbatim from the *Boeing Log Book 1916–1991* (Boeing Historical Archives, 1991) and are representative of the associated image; however, the photograph may not in every case depict the actual news item event as dated and/or described.

Unless otherwise noted, all photographs and graphics derive from the Boeing Historical Archives and are used with permission. Copyright resides with the Boeing Company. This publication has not been prepared, approved, or licensed by the Boeing Company.

INTRODUCTION

What's in a name? Wilhelm was the father of William E. Boeing and one of the many thousands of German immigrants who poured into the United States during the 1800s in search of a better life. Wilhelm arrived in America with the German surname of Böing, with an umlaut over the letter o; however, he changed the spelling to "Boeing" upon discovering there were no umlauts in the English character set. The name turned out to be ideal for an airplane company: it was short, distinctive, and a moniker rarely found in the phone book.

Best of all, it was bereft of negative connotations in every major language. For example, Bing, the Microsoft search engine, translates to "illness" in parts of China, and that hurts usage. There are also a number of food-related instances.

The Boeing Company has been viable for a century. The aerospace industry is akin to a roller coaster. Periods of expansion (boom) are too often followed by sudden contraction (bust). The long-standing involvement in both commercial and military programs mitigates that cycle by facilitating the transfer of not only skilled people but also emerging technology between product lines. The corporation thrives in the global marketplace by offering a mix of cutting-edge airliners, military programs, feats in space, and other aviation services.

After some serious stumbles in recent decades, the business prognosis at Boeing is robust—a condition consistent with the ambitions, innovation, business acumen, and straight-arrow decency of the founder. Let's meet the aviation visionary who in 1929 said, "They will someday regard airplane travel to be as commonplace and incidental as train travel."

Born on October 1, 1881, William Edward Boeing was the only son of a self-made German immigrant. Wilhelm Boeing earned his wealth in iron ore and timber but died of influenza when young William was a mere eight years of age. His mother, the former Marie Ortmann, endowed with a generous inheritance, ensured their son would receive the best education, which included boarding school in Switzerland, followed by three years at Yale.

The self-motivated Boeing, driven to emulate the financial success of his father, relocated from Virginia to rain-soaked western Washington while still in his 20s in search of his own fortune as a timber baron. A nationwide construction boom then under way stimulated the demand for lumber, and William "Bill" Boeing prospered, but life in the small coastal logging town of Hoquiam soon became mundane.

The search for excitement triggered a move to the nearby city of Seattle, where Boeing became smitten with airplanes and flying. The tall man with a mustache had the aura of an aspiring college professor with owlish eyeglasses, polished vocabulary, and carefully chosen words. Like other businessmen of that era, Boeing was most frequently photographed wearing suits and ties while stiffly posed; however, some images show him in flying attire.

The interwar period (roughly 1919 to 1937) was not only a time of complicated and dynamic business relationships but also a period of rapid innovation within the still adolescent business of aviation. Boeing chided his engineers: "Let no improvement in flying and flying equipment pass us by." Improved technology made its way back and forth between civil and military designs. Airframe materials shifted from wood and cloth to metal. A single cantilevered wing replaced bi-wings, wires, and braces. Engines became more powerful, and their reliability improved.

The decade of the Roaring Twenties was wild and crazy. It was a time of business expansion and great prosperity as speculation in securities ran rampant. Out of this cauldron of chaos emerged the monumental transportation, technological, and communication innovations of that decade. As airline traffic grew, the number of airline passengers and pounds of air cargo soared. Interest in aviation was galvanized by Charles Lindbergh's solo crossing of the Atlantic Ocean in May 1927. Expecting to get rich, the public naively poured money (some of it borrowed) into all types of securities. In turn, financiers responded by creating more opportunities for speculation.

The resulting inevitable crash of the stock market came on Black Tuesday in October 1929. Average investors were devastated, while business continued pretty much as normal for the top echelon of industrialists. It was all very complicated, and powerful Washington, DC, politicians, who had grown suspicious of the financiers and their consortia, were beginning to take note.

A controversial piece of jurisprudence called the Air Mail Act of 1934 was to henceforth change the paradigm of the aviation industry. Future justice of the Supreme Court and erstwhile senator from Alabama Hugo Black enlisted a cadre of politically motivated and like-minded anti–big business colleagues to help him investigate. Delving further into the alleged causes of the current economic malaise and the search for scapegoats would make for great political theater.

Senate investigator A.B. Patterson had prepared for William Boeing and his companies a three-page typed interrogatory with 38 wide-ranging questions that broadly probed into all aspects of the businesses. Boeing's staff did their best on short notice to gather responses to questions that were sometimes ambiguous. The public hearings took place at the Senate offices in Washington, DC. Various other airline and related industry executives were also subpoenaed.

Senator Black's technique was to persuade witnesses that he already had the facts and merely wanted confirmation for the records. Courteous, smiling, puffing gravely on his cigar, Black, a savvy and experienced prosecuting attorney, set about to refresh their memories during the review, leading them to admissions that enabled him to conclude with damaging summations of their testimony.

William Boeing's testimony began at 10:30 a.m. on February 6, 1934, and went on for hours. Unlike with pesky newspaper reporters, refusal to answer committee questions was not an option. The hearings turned into an inquisition. Boeing, who was unfamiliar with the minor nuances of the written answers prepared by others, frequently stumbled under the verbal assault. Black led the tag team of questioners, with senators Wallace White Jr. (Maine) and Patrick McCarran (Nevada) sometimes chiming in.

The investigative process, which resembled a prosecution, did not provide for a defense attorney to run interference for the witness by interjecting objections. William Boeing was a private man of means who was proud of his hard-won business accomplishments. The die had been cast. Boeing was fed up and about to forever forsake every aspect of the aviation industry, as seen in the following news item from September 18, 1934: "William E. Boeing resigns as board chairman. He sells his stock, leaves the airplane business and moves on to investments and thoroughbred horse racing."

8

One

PACIFIC AERO PRODUCTS COMPANY

Boeing was a gregarious individual who gravitated toward others with talent, education, and accomplishment. He first partnered with naval officer Conrad Westervelt (1879–1956), a graduate of the US Naval Academy and the Massachusetts Institute of Technology (MIT). Marine architects and engineers were commonly found on the payroll of the early airplane companies. The science of aeronautical engineering was still in its infancy but evolving quickly.

In 1916, an airplane company was established in the previous Heath shipyard, snugly situated on Duwamish riverfront land a short distance south of Seattle's Elliott Bay. A separate hangar was built on the shores of Lake Union. The broadly written articles of incorporation for Pacific Aero Products Company (dated July 15, 1916) established three King County residents as the principals: William Boeing, James Foley, and Edgar Gott.

A diverse crew was hired: men with woodworking skills, women who were experts at sewing, and an American-educated Chinese aeronautical engineer named Wong Tsoo (sometimes written Tsu Wong). The first airplane built was dubbed the B&W (for Boeing & Westervelt). The freshly varnished wing spars were fabricated from spruce, which was abundant on the Boeing-owned timberlands.

It was Westervelt who interviewed Wong Tsoo at MIT before penning a letter to Bill Boeing describing the attributes of the young Asian aeronautical engineer. Tsoo was familiar with the MIT wind tunnel, and Boeing wanted that expertise at his disposal. Boeing responded with a telegram, which (in part) directed, "Engage Chinaman." With these two words, the first engineer had been hired. Tens of thousands of other engineers would follow Tsoo onto the Boeing payroll over the next century.

Meanwhile, the enterprise back in Seattle thrived on wartime demand. The business was rebranded as the Boeing Airplane Company on May 9, 1917, with William Boeing firmly in control as the undisputed first CEO. Nine other men have since followed in that role.

The first two airplanes were designated as B&W (for Boeing & Westervelt). They were quickly followed by a Navy order for Model C, an airplane with a similar appearance. Lake Union is a small freshwater body in the heart of Seattle with sheltered waters ideal for flight-testing such fragile aircraft.

One of the oldest photographs in the Boeing Historical Archives depicts the sewing room. Cotton muslin fabric covered the wooden airframes. Those highly skilled in sewing were most often women. The fabric was then covered in dope to make it rigid and rain resistant.

Westervelt's highly anticipated role in the business evaporated when the Navy assigned him back East in 1916. His resignation as a naval officer was refused because of the looming war in Europe. It was Westervelt who discovered Wong Tsoo (below) at MIT and recommended him to William Boeing for hire. Westervelt's aptitude for aircraft manufacturing later came to fruition when he commanded the Naval Aircraft Factory in Philadelphia from 1921 to 1927.

The following news item was reported on March 3, 1919: "William Boeing and pilot Eddie Hubbard fly 60 letters from Vancouver, British Columbia, to Seattle in Boeing's C-700 as part of the Canadian Exposition. This is the first international airmail to reach the United States." A seed was planted in the fertile and entrepreneurial mind of William Boeing. He would build airplanes (and acquire them from others) and utilize them to transport mail at a profit. Passengers and freight soon followed.

Two

EARLY YEARS

As the demand for military airplanes waned with the end of World War I, the fledgling Boeing Airplane Company was soon building airplanes for the early mail routes. Starting in March 1919, William Boeing teamed with Eddie Hubbard to demonstrate the potential for an international airmail link between Seattle and Vancouver. Service to Victoria, the provincial capital of British Columbia, began in October 1920.

Bill Boeing became more private and reserved through the passing years, his marriage to Bertha, and the arrival of a son in late 1922. Newspaper gossip columns made occasional mention of him. A brush with Prohibition enforcement was embarrassing. Boeing sometimes declined to answer intrusive questions from the press.

In the era before defined retirement plans and corporate-sponsored health care, it was common for skilled workers to "job hop," and the Boeing people were no exception. Tsoo drifted back to China after 10 months, Foley faded from the scene, and Gott departed as president of Boeing in 1925 but later reappeared as the president of Consolidated Aircraft of San Diego.

Ten speedboats called "sea sleds" were built in 1920 at a loss of $110,123. Puget Sound adjoins Canadian waters where legal liquor flowed freely. Some of the fast square-bowed boats were rumored to be in the service of Prohibition-era rumrunners.

The web of airmail routes grew over the following years until the main corridor extended from New York to San Francisco, with ever-expanding branches reaching into many locales. Early airmail pilots took note of individuals who presented themselves at the airfields seeking transportation. When circumstances permitted, an occasional passenger would sit amid the sacks of mail in exchange for fare. Boeing observed, "People want to ride in airplanes more and more each day. I looked forward to the time when passengers would become of primary importance."

An airplane company also needed office space for engineering, purchasing, correspondence, and accountants. Wood frame buildings were common in the Northwest because large trees were nearby and abundant.

This Model C is prepared for winching into the Lake Union hangar. The pilots do not want wet feet, so they will stay aboard until the floatplane is secured indoors. The Navy was the customer for the Model C.

The following news item was reported in November 1919: "The Boeing Airplane Company struggles through most of the year with only 80 people on the payroll in Seattle. Fortunately a contract to re-model the British-designed Liberty airplane, the de Havilland DH-4, gets the company back into the airplane business as workers start rebuilding the first 50 of the fighters. The fuel tank is moved to lower the risk of fire. During the next five-years, Boeing will rebuild 298 de Havillands."

Inspired by the Fokker D.VII of World War I, the Boeing Model 15 first flew in 1923. The Navy/Marines version was designated "FB" and 44 were built. The Army version was PW-9 and 113 were delivered.

DRESSING TABLE
SUITE 100

Sometimes there were insufficient orders to keep all employees busy. Boeing would then assign men with woodworking skills to construct furniture for household use. Personal funds were used to cover any resulting operating deficit. The goal was keeping good people employed until new airplane contracts were finalized. Authentic Boeing-built furniture remains coveted by antique collectors in the Seattle area.

Chifforette # 100
Top 20 x 34

Military orders remained important in the mid-1920s. A trio of Marine Corps F4B aircraft cruise in tight formation. In Army service, the same airplane was a P-12. At this time, Boeing was a builder of small airplanes. That would change in the future.

Passengers climb aboard a Ford Tri-Motor operated by Pacific Air Transport at Seattle's Boeing Field. The Ford had two innovations: all metal construction and an enclosed cockpit. Ford Motor Company built 199 of the type between 1925 and 1933. Ford would not build any more airplanes until the arrival of World War II, when B-24s were fabricated at Willow Run.

Airmail turned out to be lucrative. Early transport aircraft like the Model 40 were designed for that specific purpose. William Boeing's income during this period derived from aircraft manufacturing, airmail contracts, and logging the coastal timberlands he continued to hold. In addition to a fine home, Boeing owned a succession of yachts, each named *Taconite*, and a series of personal airplanes, which later included a Douglas DC-5. The formal name for Boeing Field is King County International Airport. It was never owned by either the Boeing family or the Boeing Company.

The following news item was reported in 1928: "William Boeing buys Pacific Air Transport and takes over airline routes down the coast. Meanwhile, Boeing engineers design the 12-passenger three-engine biplane, the Model 80. It is the first Boeing plane built specifically as a passenger transport. July 27 – The Model 80 [above] makes its first flight. Four are built with the first being delivered to Boeing Air Transport on August 8. The design is upgraded and production continues on the 18-passenger Model 80A." The sun is low to the horizon in the image below, where crew members are shown wearing goggles to protect from bugs. On September 16, 1929, another news item was reported: "The Boeing School of Aeronautics is established in Oakland, California, to train pilots and ground crews for Boeing operated concerns."

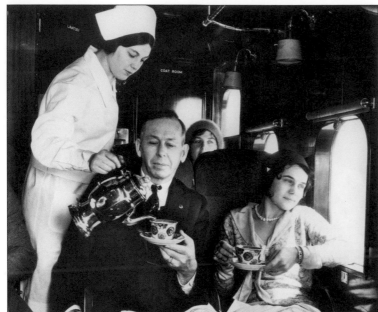

The following news item was reported on May 15, 1930: "Ellen Church, who has convinced Boeing management to use registered nurses as female flight attendants, joins the crew of a Model 80A headed to San Francisco. Using female flight attendants soon will be a universal practice."

This Model 80 interior has been converted from passenger service into en route mail sorting. It was common for railroad passenger trains to haul Railroad Post Office cars (or RPOs) where mail would be sorted in transit. The short transit times, in-flight turbulence, and greater operating expense likely doomed this experiment.

Mickey, Minnie, and Santa Claus pose in a United Air Lines Model 247. Walt Disney was working on the six-minute animated film *Plane Crazy* in 1928–1929, and this publicity photograph was likely tied to that production. Disneyland did not open until 1955, so they obviously were not flying there.

The totem logo was inspired by the many Native American totem poles found in the Pacific Northwest. Starting in 1928, the logo appeared not only on Boeing airliners but also among its advertising and manufactured products. It was also called the "bug" because of its insect-like attributes. The script version of the word *Boeing* arrived later, and the "stratotype" style (similar to italics) debuted in 1947.

The Boeing bug found its way onto this rudder. The corporate logo and image are carefully nurtured. Later, when retired, the totem pole–derived image was relegated to only historic uses, such as service pins for long-serving employees.

Western Washington is dominated by the 14,400-foot dormant volcano known as Mount Rainier. For a century, its glacier-gouged flanks have been the preferred backdrop for aerial photography of each new fixed-wing flying marvel bearing the Boeing brand name. The following news item was reported on October 5, 1929: "The Model 40B-4 makes its first flight. This is the first plane in the Model 40 series to use the two-way radio, designed by Thorpe Hiscock, William Boeing's brother-in-law."

An airplane in the sky over small-town America was an attention grabber during the first half of the 20th century. Feats of aviation in the form of "bigger, higher, and faster" were extensively covered in print, movie newsreels, and radio.

The handwritten note in the corner of this photograph reads, "Here is to Boeing Air Transport on my arrival at San Francisco July 2, 1927 as the first passenger to travel on the transcontinental service. Jane Eads." Eads was a plucky crime scene reporter for the Chicago *Herald & Examiner*, a Hearst newspaper. She turned over handwritten accounts of her journey to local reporters at each stop along the route for transcription by the wire service.

The following news item was reported on June 30, 1927: "Boeing Air Transport, Inc. (BAT) is formed to run the airline with Philip G. Johnson as president, Claire L. Egtvedt, general manager and William E. Boeing as Chairman of the Board. BAT also trains pilots, sets up airfields, and staffs maintenance facilities for the new airmail service." BAT management collaborated with the Hearst newspapers to ensure publicity. Reporter Jane Eads won the assignment as the first BAT transcontinental passenger.

Three

GREAT DEPRESSION

William Boeing was the founder and mastermind behind the biggest and most formidable of the aviation consortia. Boeing had a sharp eye for sizing up people and businesses. When he encountered exceptional men of vision and organizational ability, he recruited and mentored them.

The business expanded into other aviation endeavors far from Seattle as aviation companies of every ilk were acquired. The Chicago-based branch of the business became United Air Lines. The capstone of the Boeing corporate pyramid was United Aircraft and Transport Corporation. An empire was created in 1929 when the Boeing firms teamed up with Frederick Rentschler of Pratt & Whitney. William Boeing liked doing business with the ebullient Rentschler, but sensing a monopoly in the making, some officials in the federal government looked askance.

Implementation of the Air Mail Act of 1934 created a fiasco when Army Air Corps pilots were ordered to transport airmail. The Roosevelt administration's "New Dealers" received their first black eye when a dozen military pilots died in airplane crashes. William E. Boeing was totally innocent of any criminal act, but his pride was wounded beyond repair by the tawdry, humiliating experience of the Senate hearings and the new law. His parting words were: "I am retiring from active service in aircraft manufacturing and air transportation . . . The many forward projects now in the making will continue to keep me on the sidelines as a keen and interested observer."

All his aviation-related holdings were sold in disgust. At the age of 53, William Boeing redirected his formidable mind toward real estate development, horse breeding, and other leisure activities. It remains unknown if he harbored plans for early retirement before the hearings.

There would be no more Boeing family ownership or significant involvement in the companies he founded. The capable associates whom Boeing had handpicked and trained took charge of the three now independent companies: United Air Lines, United Aircraft Corporation (e.g., Pratt & Whitney engines), and the Boeing Airplane Company. Infused with fresh blood, each of the businesses not only survived but also went on to greater prosperity as they each came to dominate their respective markets in the coming decades.

The following news item was reported in 1929: "William E. Boeing commences an acquisition program with Chance Vought Corporation on February 28, Hamilton Metalplane Division on March 5; Boeing Aircraft of Canada in May; Stout Airlines, June 30; Northrop Aircraft Corporation, Ltd., August 12; Stearman Aircraft Co., August 15; Sikorsky Aviation Corporation, August 31; Standard Steel Propeller Company, September; and the Pratt & Whitney Aircraft Company on October 11, 1929." William Boeing (right) liked doing business with Frederick Rentschler (1887–1956), the top executive at engine builder Pratt & Whitney.

Claire Egtvedt and Philip Johnson joined Boeing in June 1917 as freshly graduated engineers from the University of Washington. Both men later rose to the top executive positions at Boeing. Pictured in 1930 beside a Boeing P-12B fighter are, from left to right, Egtvedt, General Carl A. "Tooey" Spaatz, Oliver P. Gothlin, and Lt. Robert Israel. Egtvedt was seeking customer input.

The Monomail was the first all-metal, cantilevered single-wing airplane with provisions for both mail and passengers. Only two were built and evaluated, then put into transcontinental airline service. They were hampered by a single engine and propeller constraints of the era. The B-9 bomber was derived from this design.

The P-26 Peashooter was the last fighter completely designed and built by Boeing to emerge from plants in the Puget Sound area. A total of 151 were built at a unit cost of $14,009. Only big airplanes, including bombers, tankers, and transports (both civilian and military), would follow this spunky model.

Nothing in the skies during 1937 looked bigger than the experimental XB-15. Only one was built. It was evaluated by Army Air Forces, then relegated to transport duties with the new designation of XC-105. It was scrapped in Panama in 1945. The wing design was carried forward to the Model 314.

Boeing Model 247 is considered the first "modern" airliner by featuring all-metal construction and a single cantilevered wing. All early production was earmarked for Boeing affiliate United Air Lines. Therefore, Jack Frye of TWA was compelled to take his business to Donald Douglas. Starting in 1933, a modest 75 aircraft of the Model 247 were built.

Donald Douglas (1892–1981, right) was the founder and driving force behind Douglas Aircraft Company. An intense rivalry developed between Douglas and Boeing as each company strove to win over the airliner market. The Model 247 was quickly made obsolete by the DC-3 (C-47 in military service). It and follow-on designs in the DC (Douglas Commercial) series enabled the Southern California firm to retain a 60 percent market share well into the 1950s. DC-3 production totaled 607, while the number of C-47s built exceeded 10,000.

Model 307 was a valiant attempt to win airline business. The four-engine aircraft was pressurized for passenger comfort and intended to fly at higher altitudes—above the weather that could cause discomfort. The wing and engines were borrowed from the B-17.

A Model 307 is displayed at the Smithsonian Air and Space Museum's Udvar-Hazy Center at Dulles airport. Lunchtime diners at Salty's Alki Restaurant ran for their lives on March 28, 2002, when it ingloriously ran out of fuel on a test flight and ditched into Seattle's Elliott Bay. Fortunately, it was retrieved, rinsed in fresh water, polished, and repaired to fly again.

Eddie Allen beams as he boards the Boeing Clipper. With a wingspan of 152 feet and an opulent interior, it was the biggest and classiest airliner of the day. With the outbreak of World War II, the government ordered airliner production at Boeing to halt, as bombers were prioritized.

Elsie Bachmann is shown drilling. The following news item was reported in January 1937: "The first Boeing sick leave plan is introduced. This will pay workers who miss work for a long period of time because of illness. By June, the company will have paid out $1,100 to 11 recipients. Employment high for 1937 is 1,890."

The following news item was reported on May 31, 1938: "The first Boeing Clipper (Model 314) is barged down the Duwamish Waterway for the start of preflight testing. Test pilot Eddie Allen will take the Clipper on it first flight just after 10 a.m. on June 7." Allen reported there was plenty of power, but better turning was needed. The single vertical stabilizer was then replaced with a triple tail. The small fleet of 12 Model 314s accomplished 4,100 wartime transoceanic crossings. Unfortunately, none survive. Pres. Franklin Roosevelt was aboard one of them in 1943. The experience of flying made him giddy.

Model 314 set the standard for luxury travel before and during World War II; however, the airplane was slow. One account sets the travel time from Hawaii to San Francisco at 17 hours, or a leisurely 200 miles per hour. The *Pacific Clipper* was in Auckland, New Zealand, in December 1941. In accordance with emergency orders, Capt. Robert Ford and his Pan American Airways crew successfully returned it to New York via a three-week journey, which included crossing Africa, thus making an around-the-world flight.

The following news item was reported on August 20, 1935: "Test pilot Les Tower flies the Model 299 nonstop from Seattle to Dayton, Ohio, establishing an unofficial record of 2,100 miles at an average speed of 232 miles per hour. After landing, he credits the newly designed automatic pilot with flying the plane 'most of the way.'"

The following news item was reported on October 30, 1935: "The Model 299, with a military pilot at the helm, crashes at Wright Field in Dayton, Ohio. Test pilot Les Tower (an observer on the flight) dies from burns suffered in the crash, and the $432,034 airplane is destroyed. Despite this accident, the Army will order 13 *Flying Fortresses*." (Eventually, 12,731 were built.)

Four

WORLD WAR II

The Boeing Company struggled to break into the airliner business in the decades following the 1920s but was repeatedly stymied by Douglas Aircraft Company (and sometimes by Lockheed). The surge in bomber business at Boeing started with the iconic B-17 design in 1935. Amazed at its size, a newspaper reporter quickly dubbed it a "Flying Fortress," and the name stuck.

Disaster intervened. The prototype B-17 (Model 299) was flying for evaluation purposes at Wright Field on October 30, 1935. Confusion ensued when the military pilot agreed to take additional observers aloft as other crew members were installing "gust locks." These devices prevent control surfaces from damaging movements caused by the wind when the airplane is parked outdoors and unattended.

The only Model 299 prototype crashed in flames on takeoff because the control surfaces were inoperable. Two passengers died of burns, while other onboard observers were injured but survived. The consequence was two vital safety conventions that have withstood the test of time: checklists, and an obligatory visual inspection of the aircraft by flight crew as part of the preflight ritual.

The Army Air Corps procurement officers at Wright Field in Dayton, Ohio, were more interested in economy and selected the competing Douglas B-18 Bolo. The B-18, a DC-3 derivative, promised lower unit acquisition and operating costs but failed to play a combat role in World War II. A token order for B-17s was enough to establish production while buying time to undertake the needed engineering improvements.

The B-17 decisively demonstrated Boeing's acumen with heavy bombers. This success earned Boeing the award of a massive contract to design the B-29 Superfortress, an offensive behemoth with the payload, range, and speed needed to rain destruction upon the Japanese home islands. B-29s were assembled in Renton and Wichita (by Boeing), Marietta (by Bell), and Omaha (by Martin).

The following news item was reported on September 2, 1941: "The Austin Construction Company starts work at the Renton site. More than 450,000 yards of fill will be needed to reclaim the wetlands." In this view, sawtooth factory buildings are on the left, the Cedar River is in the center, and the short (but wide) runway is on the right. Finished B-29s are also visible in this image dated May 5, 1945.

The following news item was reported on July 9, 1942: "The only XPBB-1 Sea Ranger (Model 344) long-range seaplane patrol bomber to be built by Boeing makes its first test flight. It will be nicknamed the 'Lone Ranger' because no more are built." The Navy instead opted for land-based B-25 aircraft (PBJ in Navy service), built by North American Aviation at Kansas City, and the Renton plant was reallocated for B-29 assembly.

Lt. Gen. William Knutsen (left) joins Philip Johnson (hands in pockets) in the B-17 engine shop on April 12, 1942. Knutsen, a former automobile executive and the only person in history to go from civilian to three-star general, represents an Army desperate for more heavy bombers. The following news item was reported on September 14, 1944: "Boeing President Philip G. Johnson dies of a stroke in Wichita. The board starts looking for a new president."

The following news item was reported in 1943: "Burlap buildings and chicken-wire lawns camouflage Seattle's Plant 2 so that it looks like a quiet suburb from the air. More and more women join the company ranks. By December, they will make up 46 percent of the workforce."

Above is the cockpit of a B-17, which could fly in the stratosphere but lacked pressurization. Crew members inhale aviator's oxygen in a preflight process called "denitrogenizing," as seen below. The goal is to reduce the amount of nitrogen in the body to decrease the probability that life-threatening gaseous bubbles will form at high altitudes.

Cooks in the cafeteria kitchen prepare lunch while workers take a break. The Department of Agriculture wanted a photograph depicting healthy eating, hence the workers munching on apples and drinking milk. Employees were an invaluable resource to the war effort. Employers strove to keep them happy so they would not quit and take their valuable job skills elsewhere. Employee assistance programs began during the war years, when having loved ones away at war and spending long hours in a factory could drive a person to tears.

The following news item was reported in 1944: "Around the clock, the war effort keeps going, and companies throughout North America have been subcontracted to build parts for the bombers. Workers are sent out to recruit other workers. Payroll skyrockets. Almost a fifth of Seattle's population is involved with Boeing work. In March alone, the company turns out 362 B-17s." Boeing and other wartime aircraft producers utilized a production innovation called "feeder plants." Workers in nearby communities toiled in rented space suitable for factory work to fabricate subassemblies, which were then transported to the final-assembly site.

Workers at Seattle's Plant 2 celebrated the 5,000th B-17. They were invited to conspicuously sign their names on the finished product, and it then became known as the "Five Grand." In the era before electronic computers, automobile-style assembly-line techniques were applied to production, which peaked at 15 airplanes per day. Most heavy bombers were named by their flight crews and adorned on their forward flanks with sometimes-racy artwork of scantily clad women in a genre called nose art. The military was eager to keep defense workers happy and motivated.

The most expensive project of World War II was the B-29 Superfortress. The rushed project was fraught with serious engineering and manufacturing challenges, as seen in the following news item from February 18, 1943: "The crash of the second experimental model XB-29 bomber in Seattle killed test pilot and chief aerodynamicist Eddie Allen and the crew." Two months later, on April 15, 1943, another news item was reported as follows: "Boeing Wichita Division completes its first production model B-29."

World War II–era airplanes were most often made of metal and held together by thousands of fasteners, which were primarily rivets. Holes needed to be drilled first, with riveting to follow. Riveting was a two-person task. One person, the bucker, held a heavy metal weight while the other operated the rivet gun to pound a rounded head onto the soft metal, thus ensuring a tight fit.

The B-17 bristled with .50-caliber Browning machine guns. The B-17 was beloved by aircrews for its ability to absorb battle damage, maintain tight formation, and provide mutual defense against fighter aircraft.

Hydraulic systems utilize oil under pressure to reliably raise and lower landing gear and move other control surfaces. Quality control inspectors hover over each aspect of airplane production. Mistakes in aircraft assembly are never acceptable. Each moving part was bench-tested before installation.

Like fraternal twins, the last KC-97 (left) has been pushed from the factory while the first KC-135 (lower), bearing tail number 55-3118, emerges into the sunshine as a band plays music on July 18, 1956. The music would be momentarily overwhelmed by the roar of a dozen J-57 jet engines as the Dash 80 prototype led a B-52 on a low west-to-east flyby overhead. The military might of the United States was significantly enhanced by these products, which endured for many decades.

Five

COLD WAR

According to a news item from August 15, 1945, "The war is over. The government terminates its order for 581 B-29As. Other terminations will cut production to five airplanes monthly by the end of 1946. More than 30,000 Boeing workers are left without jobs. William Allen was the aviation visionary who replaced Philip Johnson as Boeing president on September 1, 1945.

Four important products kept the Boeing facilities busy and profitable during the Cold War era. First to fly was the six-engine B-47 in 1947, followed by the legendary B-52 Stratofortress. The big bomber needed aerial refueling from an aircraft with the speed, altitude, and capacity to sate a behemoth powered by eight fuel-thirsty jet engines. The KC-135 Stratotanker fit the requirement perfectly. The Minuteman intercontinental nuclear-tipped missile rounded out the Strategic Air Command's nuclear force and augmented the nation's submarine-launched missile fleet.

William Allen (1900–1985) knew the halcyon days of designing and building big bombers was waning, as seen in the following news item from May 20, 1952: "Unable to get others to participate, and with no orders for a jet transport on the books, the company decides to use its own money to build the Model 367-80, the jetliner prototype and forerunner of the Model 707. It is constructed in a closed-off area in the Renton plant."

He bet the company on a project that (if successful) would leapfrog the propeller-driven airliners of the 1950s and best the competition. The drawings were tabbed 367-80, in a ruse to dampen internal speculation and mislead any snooping competitors. Model 367 was actually a C-97.

William Boeing and his wife, Bertha, were invited back to the company that bore their surname on May 15, 1954. The couple strode into the sprawling Renton factory in time for the 4:00 p.m. event. It was later reported that 72-year-old Boeing looked on with tears in his eyes. Despite being labeled with the words *Boeing 707* on its tail, the Dash 80 was actually more closely related to the USAF KC-135 jet tanker.

The following news item was reported in October 1948: "The experiments with inflight refueling begin with a 'trailing hose' system and continue with a 'flying boom.' This development gives bombers the intercontinental range they need and establish Boeing as a builder of tankers and receivers." (The receiver is a North American B-45.)

Open bull pens with rows of desks were common at the Boeing Company. Depending on the supervisor, attendance and breaks were rigidly enforced. Typical office hours were 7:30 a.m. to 4:00 p.m. with a 40-minute lunch.

CEO William Allen (right) discusses the future of bomber aircraft with an important visitor—Dwight "Ike" Eisenhower. The public was unaware that a secret project was under way in the adjacent factory to construct the XB-47, the first swept-wing jet-powered bomber. For public consumption, Eisenhower was photographed inspecting a conventional bomber, but covertly, he also viewed the classified XB-47.

Ike ponders as William Allen (far right) steps back to encourage his top two engineers, Ed Wells (left) and Wellwood Beall (wearing a bow tie), to speak directly to the nation's top general. The first of two news items was reported on June 5, 1946: "The Air Force officially announces that it had ordered two prototypes designated XB-47." The following statement was made on June 28, 1946: "Boeing signs a contract to design the B-52, a long-range heavy bomber."

A flight aboard a B-47 inspired William Allen, a graduate of Harvard Law School, to "bet the company" by investing $16 million into the development of the Dash-80. Douglas and Lockheed teamed up with Boeing to get over 2,000 B-47s built and into Air Force service.

Test pilot Alvin M. "Tex" Johnston (1914–1998) climbs aboard the XB-52 on October 3, 1952. The experimental airplane had been flying for about six months as engineers updated the design for the production versions, which were being rushed to defend America against the perceived Soviet nuclear threat. The tandem cockpit of the XB-52 and YB-52 gave way to a side-by-side arrangement at the insistence of Gen. Curtis Le May, the nation's top bomber general.

William Boeing, with cane in hand, sits behind William Allen as the elegant, articulate, and graceful CEO addresses the crowd on May 15, 1954. Boeing engineers knew the KC-97 (nose poking from the factory) was inadequate for midair refueling of the B-52 and that a new jet tanker was needed. In the foreground is W.P. Gwinn of jet engine builder Pratt & Whitney.

Two decades after his departure from the industry, an elderly William Boeing chats with William Allen as the pair inspects the revolutionary Model 367-80 (Dash 80 in contemporary terms) on the day it was revealed to the public. Below, Bertha Boeing christens the Model 707 prototype with champagne as the ground crew awaits the signal to tow the game-changing airplane out of the factory and into the late-afternoon sunshine. An improvised temporary steel bar protects the delicate radar dome from damage.

The term *aluminum overcast* has sometimes been jokingly used to describe an aircraft formation so large that it blots out the sun. The Air Force demonstrates its B-47 bomber muscle with a formation flyby at an air show on September 13, 1955. The location of the air show was not documented. Nuclear weapons obsolesced the large bomber formations that were often launched during World War II. It was no longer necessary to drop tons of conventional bombs to destroy large targets.

Swaggering Boeing test pilot Tex Johnston is seen here in the aircrew locker room, adjacent to the parachute loft in the B-52 hangar. Johnston had new cowboy boots fabricated before each "first flight," and they are now museum pieces. He earned fame as the pilot in command of the early B-52 and the Dash 80 flights. Major Kong, the fictional B-52 pilot portrayed by Slim Pickens in the classic 1964 film *Dr. Strangelove*, was said to be inspired by Johnston.

The following news item was reported on March 11, 1957: "The 707 prototype, or Dash 80, with members of the press on board, flies 2,350 miles non-stop from Seattle to Baltimore in the record time of 3 hours and 48 minutes at an average speed of 612 miles per hour."

CBS television news anchorman Douglas Edwards interviews fearless test pilot Tex Johnston regarding the record-setting dash from Seattle while youthful copilot Lew Wallick looks on from the left. As reported in this news item from August 7, 1955, "Tex Johnston barrel-rolls the Dash 80 over the Seafair course on Lake Washington and follows that maneuver with a second roll. This antic causes great consternation among watching Boeing executives."

Extreme braking during refused takeoff (RTO) testing of the Dash 80 yielded a fire. Foam was used to extinguish the flames, but the aftermath is clearly evident. The airplane is loaded to maximum weight, worn-down brakes and tires are installed, and the airplane is then brought to maximum speed before emergency braking to full stop is applied. Hazardous testing is conducted at Edwards Air Force Base in the Mojave Desert of California. RTOs are an example of the abusive treatment inflicted on test airplanes to ensure the safety of fare-paying passengers.

A KC-135Q refuels an SR-71. The Mach 3–capable SR-71 burns special fuel (grade JP7), and the body tanks in the KC-135Q are segregated from the wing tanks, which supply the tanker's engines with standard military jet fuel (grade JP4). All SR-71 aircraft are now retired but can be viewed at many aviation museums.

The first KC-135 (tail number 55-3118), dubbed the "City of Renton," reposes in the perpetual position of takeoff on static display at McConnell Air Force Base in Wichita, Kansas. Many of her younger siblings still serve in the Air Force at an advanced age as they await replacement by the KC-46 Pegasus, a military derivative of Model 767. (Author's collection.)

Frank Piasecki was an early inventor and builder of helicopters. His company Vertol (for Vertical Takeoff and Landing) was located in suburban Philadelphia. The following news item was reported on March 31, 1960: "Boeing acquires Vertol Aircraft Corporation and its subsidiaries. Vertol has been awarded a $19 million Army contract for its Model 114, the Chinook helicopter." The Chinook debuted during the Vietnam War and remains a star performer.

At peak, over 1,000 Minuteman intercontinental ballistic missiles were sheltered in underground silos across the northern tier of America. They could launch on short notice to inflict nuclear havoc on faraway targets. Two unarmed missiles were launched from Vandenberg Air Force Base to streak across the Pacific on a test flight. Viability of the weapons system was demonstrated when operational missiles were selected at random, then disarmed and flown to Vandenberg Air Force Base, where they were launched toward a target in the Kwajalein Test Range.

The LGM-30 Minuteman missile is raised to a vertical position by a special transporter truck. The 78,000-pound missile is then lowered into its underground silo. Solid fuel enables it to remain ready for instant launch while unattended for extended periods of time. Air Force officers hunker down in nearby underground launch control facilities, ready to respond to a doomsday order, which must originate from the president of the United States.

A B-52 mother ship drops an X-15 over California. North American Aviation built the X-15 for the US Air Force and NASA to probe the boundaries of space in the late 1950s. The B-52 carried it into the stratosphere, where rocket motors drove it much higher. X-15 pilots wore astronaut wings.

With 8 engines, 12 fuel tanks, and a gaggle of hydraulic and electrical systems to manage, the B-52 was amazingly built without a flight engineer's position. Because of its ample electrical supply and plenty of space in the aft fuselage, many upgrades have been integrated into the B-52 as technology has advanced over the decades.

A freshly built B-52H with wing-mounted Skybolt missiles reposes in the Wichita sunshine. The B-52H was the only model with more powerful turbo-fan engines and the only version remaining combat ready. The following news item was reported on June 22, 1962: "The last B-52H rolls out in Wichita, to be delivered to the Air Force on October 26. This will mark the end of B-52 production. Since 1951, a total of 467 B-52s were built at Wichita and 277 in Seattle."

This photograph has been labeled to show the 32 feet of normal flex built into the B-52 wing. Outrigger wheels near the wingtip prevent the wings from hitting the ground. With a wingspan of 185 feet, routine B-52 operations require a long, paved runway with a minimum width of 200 feet. The B-52 lacks outboard ailerons because of the extreme wing flex. Instead, spoilers are used to dampen roll and maintain level flight. Heavy steel rigs like this are used to test aircraft wings to destruction. Depending on the model, they sometimes break at about 150 percent of the design limit.

Munitions handlers at U-Tapao Airfield in Thailand work in tropical rain to load 60,000 pounds of conventional bombs onto this B-52D around 1972–1973. The older D models were downgraded from nuclear duties, modified, and dispatched to the Pacific during the Vietnam War. The B-52D was reliable and easy to maintain, even when flying daily bombing sorties. An enlisted tail gunner operated a quartet of lethal .50-caliber machine guns. There are two documented instances where the tail guns destroyed enemy MiG fighters during air-to-air combat. (Both, author's collection.)

The B-52 has been battle-tested in multiple conflicts. During the Vietnam War, they normally flew in three-ship formations and were sometimes joined over the target by other bombers arriving from Guam, along with smaller support aircraft operating from nearby bases. Midair refueling was provided (as needed) by KC-135 aircraft, often flying from U-Tapao Airfield in Thailand or Kadena Air Base in Japan. The sun rises on another hot day in the tropics as this B-52D safely returns from a night mission.

The race to the moon was an extension of the Cold War. The following news item was reported in October 1969: "Boeing starts building the Lunar Roving Vehicle, a four-wheeled motorcar to be used by astronauts on the Moon. The company will complete delivery of the first three working vehicles within 17 months." Boeing was one of several contractors who collaborated to build the Saturn V liquid-fueled launch vehicle with the necessary thrust to deliver humans (and the hardware to keep them alive) to the moon and return them safely to earth. Boeing stepped forward to perform important behind-the-scenes management tasks for NASA after a fatal fire on an earthbound Apollo capsule in 1967. The concurrent 747, 737, SST, and moon-landing projects stretched Boeing resources thin in the late 1960s.

The Air Force received 45 C-135A jet transports (a Model 717-157 was sans refueling equipment) for interim airlift of passengers and cargo pending delivery of the C-141 Starlifter from Lockheed. Meanwhile, a Model 707 in Air Force service went by several designations, one of which was VC-137.

From 1936 to 2001, Boeing corporate headquarters were located in south Seattle behind an unpretentious Art Deco facade fronted by a railroad spur. The original 2-24 building (shown here) was deemed inadequate for earthquakes and was torn down before corporate headquarters moved into the former Morton Salt building in downtown Chicago.

As seen here in 1953, Plant 2 retained most of its World War II configuration. The employee cafeteria (lower center) has an arched roof. Office space is provided in the engineering building. Sawtooth factory buildings allowed natural light to enter. Boeing Field is east of Highway 99, and the plant is to the west. The Duwamish River flows behind. Like many old factories, the site was contaminated with hydrocarbons, and cleanup tasks are ongoing.

The Model 377 Stratoliner evolved from the B-29 design and was Boeing's first postwar attempt to penetrate the commercial market. With stiff competition from Douglas and Lockheed, airline sales were anemic (only 56 sold); however, military orders for both tanker and transport versions boosted production. The upper and lower lobes of this Stratoliner are evident as the aft fuselage is being assembled.

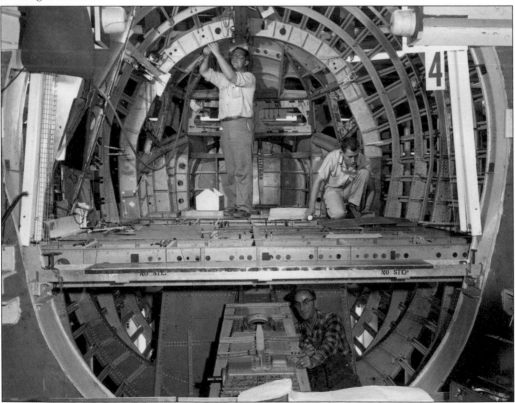

A hangar covering five acres was constructed to host the B-52 flight-test program. Formally known as the 3-390 Building, the structure was more commonly referred to as the B-52 Hangar for decades thereafter. A cantilevered roof allows all the doors on the east side to open simultaneously. It remains a busy place frequented by exciting new airplanes of the latest design.

A Boeing flight crew scans their checklist as they prepare to take the Dash 80 aloft. It cruised alone in the stratosphere high above the North Atlantic Ocean to determine the best routes and flying times between major destinations as airlines made preparations for delivery of their first production 707s.

The navigator, radio operator, and flight engineer flight crew positions were gradually eliminated through the invention of newer and better systems. Elimination of these positions reduced airline labor expense while simultaneously increasing the amount of revenue-generating space within the airframe. Modern jets are operated by a pilot and copilot; however, crews are augmented on the longest flights to allow for rest in compartments that are hidden away from passenger view.

Six

JET AGE

The Dash 80 immediately went to work as a flight-test workhorse based at Seattle's Boeing Field until retirement in 1972. On March 11, 1957, it set a long-standing speed record by making a nonstop dash from Seattle to Baltimore in a blistering 3 hours and 48 minutes. It also roamed the inky-black subzero skies of the North Atlantic alone in the stratosphere as it established routes, altitudes, and en route times while the world's elite flyers awaited the arrival of the first Boeing 707 airliners.

Intense airliner competition with the Douglas DC-8 forced Boeing to make subtle but drastic changes to the Dash 80 design. First, the airlines lobbied for six-abreast seating in coach class, which remains today; therefore, the fuselage was widened. Second, the airlines demanded speed, range, and efficiency improvements, so the wing was redesigned. A reengineered fuselage mated to a newly designed wing yielded a new airplane. These improvements distinguish Model 707 from the KC-135 (Model 717).

The surviving Dash 80 is proudly displayed at the Smithsonian's Udvar-Hazy Center at Dulles airport, where it shares the floor with two older sisters: a shiny Model 307 sporting an exterior of polished aluminum, and the *Enola Gay*, the B-29 that dropped the first atomic bomb on Japan in 1945. The Dash 80 paved the way for a parade of constantly evolving transport aircraft designs that continues to this day. The different models vary in size and configuration. The concept of jet engines in pods under swept wings remains the common denominator, yielding the efficient, reliable, and affordable air transportation now enjoyed by the traveling public worldwide.

A string of new models flowed from Boeing as engineers probed various possible combinations of fuselage sizes, interacting with the number, thrust, and location of engines in search of the optimum mix. Model 747 is the largest and most widely recognized by the public as the first jumbo jet. Model 737 is the smallest and most popular member of the family (as measured by unit sales). Everything else fit between the extremes, including Models 727, 757, 767, 777, and 787. Models 707, 727, and 757 have been phased out of production.

Travel aboard the early jets was a special treat when sumptuous meals were served to those attired in their finest clothing. The Airline Deregulation Act of 1978 slashed the cost of travel, eliminated most passenger perks, and destabilized the airline industry. Many airlines like Pan American, Western, Braniff, and Eastern disappeared in the wake of deregulation as the pay and benefits of airline employees were slashed.

Control tower operators oversee arrivals and departures as an early 707 in TWA livery makes a graceful departure from Los Angeles International Airport (LAX). Model 707 was one of several early competitors that quickly vanquished propeller-driven airliners from the longer routes with its greater speed and smooth ride. LAX started as Mines Field in the 1930s, then was later known as Los Angeles Municipal Airport. It is a busy hub for international service and is augmented for domestic service by other nearby regional airports in Southern California.

All Boeing single-aisle models (707, 727, 737, and 757) share the same fuselage diameter. Five-abreast seating afforded more comfortable travel; however, better economies were achieved when seats were narrowed to accommodate six seats per row. Note that the open overhead racks were for hats. Overhead luggage bins would come later.

A flight attendant graces the galley of a modern jetliner during preflight preparations. Complimentary meal service has all but vanished for economy passengers on US domestic flights; however, onboard flight attendants are required to operate the doors and direct passengers in case of an emergency. Meanwhile, beneath her feet, a smiling (but seldom photographed) baggage handler plies his craft. The cloth bags contain airmail, which, along with parcels and freight, remains an airline staple.

What look like huge science-fictional caged industrial insects on display at a zoo are actually sophisticated flight simulators used to train and qualify pilots. They can safely simulate in-flight emergencies too dangerous to undertake in actual flight. The following news item was reported on July 22, 1983: "The Federal Aviation Administration (FAA) announces that there is such a high degree of commonality between the 757 and the 767 that a pilot who qualifies on one model is automatically qualified on the other."

Boeing made massive investments in computer technology for unique business requirements, such as engineering, manufacturing, spare parts inventory, and analysis of flight-test data. Standard business functions like human resources, payroll, and finance were also computerized. Massive tape libraries were established to organize and store the thousands of reels of magnetic tape needed by the (now obsolete) computers of that time.

Model 727 followed the 707. It was intended for medium-range and shorter runways. The sleek design featured three engines, a distinctive T-tail, and triple-slotted flaps. Production halted at 1,832 units and the arrival of the 757. D.B. Cooper earned a place in infamy when he extorted bags of cash from Northwest Airlines, donned a parachute, and then jumped into inky darkness from the open ventral air-stair door of a 727 somewhere between Seattle and Portland on the evening of November 24, 1971.

The tradition of a wooden mockup of new designs was a universal step in product development before computer technology with the acronym of CATIA (computer-aided three-dimensional interactive application) eliminated the need. Mockups were constructed to ensure that multiple parts beneath the aircraft skin did not occupy the same space. CATIA arrived at Boeing with the Model 777 in the early 1990s.

A railroad switching crew has delivered a forward-fuselage section from Wichita to the 737 factory on a foggy morning. Until recently, Boeing preferred rail transportation of major sections. Assemblies for big airplanes like the 747 needed to be small enough to fit aboard a railroad car.

JT8D PRINCIPAL CHANGES

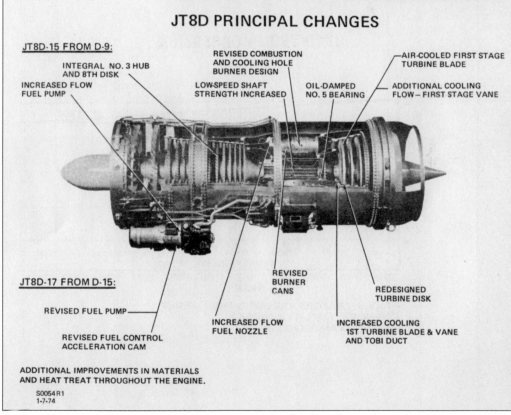

JT8D-15 FROM D-9:

INTEGRAL NO. 3 HUB AND 8TH DISK

INCREASED FLOW FUEL PUMP

REVISED COMBUSTION AND COOLING HOLE BURNER DESIGN

LOW-SPEED SHAFT STRENGTH INCREASED

OIL-DAMPED NO. 5 BEARING

AIR-COOLED FIRST STAGE TURBINE BLADE

ADDITIONAL COOLING FLOW – FIRST STAGE VANE

JT8D-17 FROM D-15:

REVISED FUEL PUMP

REVISED FUEL CONTROL ACCELERATION CAM

REVISED BURNER CANS

INCREASED FLOW FUEL NOZZLE

REDESIGNED TURBINE DISK

INCREASED COOLING 1ST TURBINE BLADE & VANE AND TOBI DUCT

ADDITIONAL IMPROVEMENTS IN MATERIALS AND HEAT TREAT THROUGHOUT THE ENGINE.

S0054R1
1-7-74

A trio of Pratt & Whitney JT8D jet engines were firmly affixed into the tail of every 727. A pair of them also powered early versions of the 737 and Douglas DC-9 regional jets. Jet engines are very expensive and normally arrive aboard dedicated semitrucks. Propulsion systems (sometimes called Power-Pack & Strut) attach the pylon and requisite wiring, tubing, cowling, and other gadgets before final assembly.

The infant 737 program was moved from Seattle to Renton during the tough times of the early 1970s. Models 707, 727, and 737 were built under the same roof, yielding the moniker of 7/7/7 Division. All the Boeing single-aisle jet airliners have been assembled in Renton; however, a new factory would be needed for the wide bodies because the ceiling cranes were too low at the Seattle, Renton, and Wichita plants.

By 1966, a total of 15 airlines had placed orders for 124 Model 737 airliners. The "Baby Boeing" was billed as the newest member of an expanding family of jets. Six-abreast seating combined with shared parts and technology from the 707 and 727 lines would yield other synergies; however, pilot union concerns regarding proper crew size put the earliest 737s at a disadvantage compared to the competing Douglas DC-9. The first flight was on April 9, 1967, followed by the first deliveries of the 737-100 to Lufthansa on December 28 and a 737-200 to United on the following day.

A replica of the c. 1916 B&W is posed adjacent to a Model 737 in this 1968 photograph. In recent decades, Boeing has revered historic aircraft. Lew Wallick's restored P-12 resided in the B-52 Hangar (3-390 Building) between flights during the 1970s.

Here, workers are shown installing sidewall panels in 1968. Airline interiors are periodically replaced over their 20-plus-year life expectancy. Overhead bins, galleys, lavatories, seats, and floor coverings all wear out when in constant service.

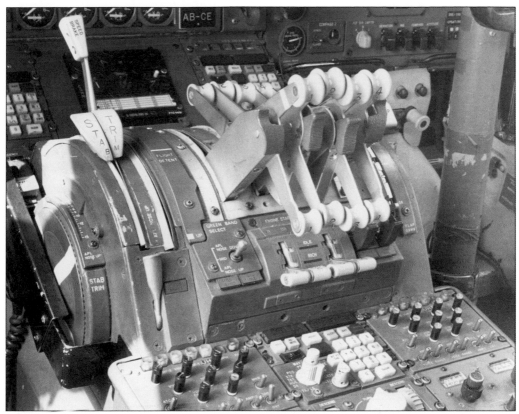

Thrust for a multiengine jet aircraft is controlled by throttles in the cockpit, conveniently located for either pilot to operate. The number of throttles corresponds to the number of engines. It can be two (as in a Model 737) or up to eight (found only in a B-52).

The noisy JT8D engines that powered all Model 727s and early versions of the 737 gave way to the CFM56-2 (and later CFM56-3) series after 727 production ceased. Each CFM56-3 engine weighs 4,278 pounds but delivers 20,000 pounds of takeoff thrust.

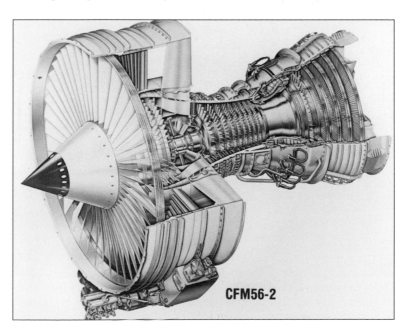

CFM56-2

A fuselage takes shape in Wichita. Stearman Aircraft of Kansas was acquired in 1929. Commercial aircraft operations were spun off to become Spirit AeroSystems in 2006. Subsequently, the remaining military manufacturing and engineering operations in Wichita were also phased out.

Overhead cranes are vital for moving large assemblies. The operator sits in a tiny cab high above everything below. A spotter on the factory floor hooks the loads and carefully coordinates all movements with the crane operator.

It is an icy-cold morning in Wichita as this railcar-mounted fuselage awaits the arrival of the locomotive, which will begin its long journey across America to the Renton factory, nestled on the shores of faraway Lake Washington. Two or three fuselages (on average) need to depart every workday to meet current production schedules. Below, new jetliners await delivery at Boeing Field around 1991. Boeing is the largest exporter in the United States.

Like automobiles, 737s now travel along a moving assembly line. Wings, fuselage, engines, and interior parts enter the factory at the south end and completed airplanes depart at the north end.

A farmer was observed lofting bales of hay into his barn using a conveyor. The agrarian-based technology was borrowed, then adapted to quickly and efficiently install passenger seats into the cabin. Exterior painting and installation of seats are the final steps before an airliner is placed into revenue service.

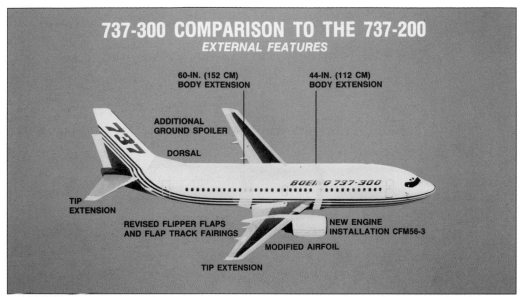

737-300 COMPARISON TO THE 737-200
EXTERNAL FEATURES

60-IN. (152 CM)
BODY EXTENSION

44-IN. (112 CM)
BODY EXTENSION

ADDITIONAL
GROUND SPOILER

DORSAL

TIP
EXTENSION

REVISED FLIPPER FLAPS
AND FLAP TRACK FAIRINGS

NEW ENGINE
INSTALLATION CFM56-3

MODIFIED AIRFOIL

TIP EXTENSION

The 737 has gone through four major iterations of design intended to keep it fresh and competitive. Dispatch reliability has been maintained at close to 100 percent, while operating cost, noise, and fuel consumption have been reduced.

Commercial airlines like choices, so the 737 is offered in various lengths, as depicted in this marketing graphic. These variants have since been superseded by newer iterations. The newest 737s have more passenger capacity but similar range as compared to the original Model 707.

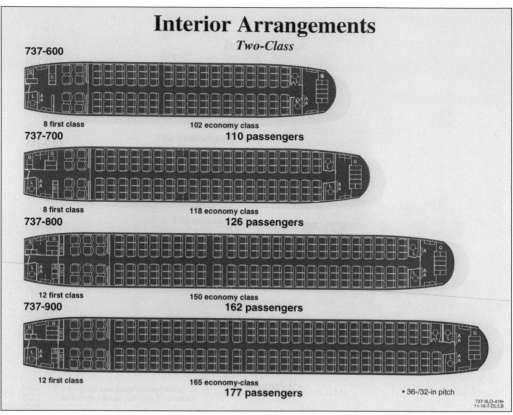

Interior Arrangements
Two-Class

737-600

8 first class   102 economy class
110 passengers

737-700

8 first class   118 economy class
126 passengers

737-800

12 first class   150 economy class
162 passengers

737-900

12 first class   165 economy-class
177 passengers   • 36-/32-in pitch

737-9LO-418•
11-16-7-DL/LB

Commercial airlines also make the choice on seating arrangements. Pitch is the distance between rows, and seat width is a function of fuselage diameter and the desired number of seats per row. Passengers have the final vote when they select an airline.

Stickers and patches are a means for employees to take pride in their project; however, aerospace work can sometimes become so schedule driven and intense that it encroaches upon home life and health. Another risk is that the project will end on a downswing in the business cycle and a layoff will follow.

The plucky Korean War–era F-86 Sabre Jet chase plane is seen as it arrived at the B-52 Hangar on December 21, 1963, after purchase from the Canadian Air Force. Fresh paint, overhaul, and modifications would transform it into a versatile performer. Boeing test pilots loved to fly chase in the F-86. Decades later, it was returned to the original Canadian livery and placed on display at the nearby Museum of Flight. If the citizens of Tacoma, Washington, had looked skyward, they would have observed the F-86 in tight formation with a 707 as options for midair refueling were probed.

Open stalls at the Seattle Delivery Center bring smiles to the accountants (when production rates are high). Deliveries bring cash to the bank account, inventory is reduced, and the demand for new airframes means airlines are prospering. It also signals a healthy factory because there is no backlog of airplanes awaiting missing parts. The following news item was reported in August 1984: "The U.S. Army Airborne Optical Adjunct project begins with Boeing as the prime contractor. This is an airborne warning system using optical sensors located in a dolphin-shaped 767, which flies at 40,000 feet." The airplane in the foreground was the first Model 767, but it was sadly scrapped when the project ended in 2002.

The Wright brothers utilized a wind tunnel, and William Boeing was quick to recognize its importance. He offered to fund a wind tunnel at the University of Washington in Seattle if the school added an aeronautical engineering program. Multiple wind tunnels and various engineering laboratories are scattered about Seattle Plant 2, where they remain staffed with (mostly) happy engineers who love their work and are vital to the never-ending advancement of aviation.

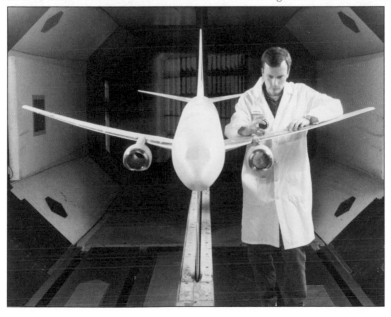

A vast forest adjacent to Paine Field in Everett, Washington, was selected as the site for the 747 factory. Perched on a 500-foot bluff above the nearby Mukilteo Harbor and rail lines, its location allowed for major assemblies to arrive by highway, rail, or sea. Therefore, the steepest rail branch in North America was constructed to loft arriving parts to the plant. Crews were trained to operate modified locomotives on an operation that could turn deadly if a railcar was to ever run away. Special railcars deliver large aircraft assemblies. When possible, the assemblies are covered to protect the soft aluminum from damage en route.

The project leader for the 747 program during the late 1960s was Joe Sutter. He became a legend for engineering excellence and was still performing valuable consulting services for Boeing well into his 90s. His autobiography, *747*, is an inspiring story and recommended reading. The Everett team earned the title of "Incredibles" while designing and building the massive airplane as the factory was being assembled around them.

Wide-bodied jets are assembled in the massive Everett plant, the largest building (by volume) in the world. The workforce at times exceeds 30,000 people, and the roof of the main factory covers about 100 acres. Models 747, 767, 777, and 787 are assembled here.

Counting the engines on this 747 would consume all the digits on one hand. There are five. Each 747 has a hard-point inboard of the No. 2 engine where a nonoperational spare engine (like an automobile spare tire) can be attached for ferrying to a remote location.

Model Debbie Stenstrom has happily shed her shoes to demonstrate the gaping maw of this Pratt & Whitney JT9D-7Q jet engine on July 17, 1979. Customers could select engines to power their 747 from Pratt & Whitney, General Electric, or Rolls-Royce. Like airframes, the competition for engine sales is fierce. The evolution of jet-turbine engines over the decades has been a legacy of less noise, more thrust, reduced fuel consumption, and increased reliability.

Senators are powerful people. Sen. William Proxmire of Wisconsin led the effort to defund the American supersonic transport (SST) in 1971. There were objections over cost, sonic boom, and environmental damage. Demand for airliners was soft, the moon landing had been accomplished, and the SST was canceled. In Seattle, the Boeing workforce fell by 70 percent, and area homes could be purchased at bargain-basement prices. In fact, a billboard in South Seattle stated, "Will the last person leaving Seattle turn out the lights." (Courtesy of the Wisconsin Historical Society, WHS-58409.)

The following news item was reported on December 31, 1966: "Boeing wins the competition to design the supersonic transport. General Electric will build the SSTs engines." Model 2707 was to be a huge airplane capable of hauling 250–300 passengers at speeds approaching Mach 3. This graphic depicts a swing-wing version with control surfaces in landing position (left) and tucked away for efficient supersonic cruise (right). The Europeans and Russians developed smaller versions, but neither was an economic success. No operational SST currently exists.

NASA-905 enters into a dive over Edwards Air Force Base to generate the lift necessary to put space shuttle *Enterprise* into flight. The concept of landing the free-falling shuttle needed to be demonstrated before flights into space could commence. The heavily modified former American Airlines 747 was the right tool for the job. Boeing was involved in a number of exciting projects during the 1970s.

Model 757 was intended to replace the 727 as both a passenger and cargo hauler. This is a concept drawing of the freighter version. It has a large cargo door and strengthened floor, but lacks fuselage windows. The following news item was reported on July 15, 1987: "The 757-PF rolls out. This version is designed specifically for the package-freight industry. It will make its first flight on August 13. United Parcel Service orders 20."

Employees at the Everett factory demonstrate their pride and interest in the upcoming rollout of Model 777 in 1994. The program was under the leadership of future Boeing CEO Phil Condit and future Ford Motor Company CEO Alan Mulally. The pair of gifted engineers preached the concept of "Working Together" to break down the invisible barriers that sometimes separate departments within a big company. The unique spotting feature of the 777 is the massive main landing gear, which has six wheels on each truck.

Be assured that this is not a beer-aging facility. The barrels aboard this Model 777 can perform two important flight-test functions: shift water with pumps to move the center of gravity during flight, and test generators by providing an electric heating element immersed in water. The barrels, all flight-test equipment, and associated wiring were removed (in a process called refurbishment) before customer delivery.

Commercial airliners have the space necessary for instrumentation and engineers to ride aboard test flights as they gather data and monitor critical stresses in real time. Boeing relies less upon telemetry than other companies because there are transmission-blocking mountains on both sides of Seattle.

A camera is rolling to capture the results of this velocity minimum unstick (VMU) test, a challenging maneuver normally performed only at Edwards Air Force Base. A hardwood-faced skid pad is attached to the lower tail before the airplane is over-rotated at slow speeds to test its ability to safely continue the takeoff. Flight-test airplanes are designated with the word *Experimental* conspicuously stenciled above the primary door.

The splash pattern of water is determined in this 1960s test of the No. 5 Model 737. Below, three decades later, the No. 4 Model 777 performs the same test. The goal of flight-testing is to obtain government certification that a new model is safe to operate in revenue service. United Airlines has been the kickoff customer for several new Boeing designs.

Boeing is excellent at creating variants of its products. Model 747SP (for Special Performance) emerged from the Everett factory on May 19, 1975. It was shorter than other 747s but had longer range and greater speed. Pan American Airways needed an airplane that could fly nonstop from New York to Tokyo. Subsequent improvements to full-size 747s eventually met and exceeded that requirement; therefore, the 747SP did not meet sales expectations.

Aero magazine, a Boeing customer service publication, made innovative use of an archival photograph in 2000 to contrast the flight crew of a historic Model 247 airliner with the flight deck of a modern wide-body. It depicts the massive growth of airliners while retaining the timeless bond between pilot and copilot as they collaborate to ply their assigned pathways in the sky.

Two YC-14 aircraft first flew in 1976 under an Air Force initiative to replace the Lockheed C-130 Hercules tactical airlifter. The airplane featured twin 747-type engines, upper-surface blown flaps, and other innovations. The competing McDonnell-Douglas YC-15 grew and evolved into the very successful C-17 Globemaster III airlifter, while the C-130J remains in production at Lockheed Martin's Marietta plant in Georgia.

Seven

LAST SUPPER

In 1993, Secretary of Defense William Perry invited senior executives from the defense contractors to Washington, DC. The event later became known as the "last supper." In the wake of the collapse of the Soviet empire, the industrialists were informed that the Department of Defense (DoD) would no longer ensure their survival by awarding contracts to all of them. The administration of Pres. William Clinton was reaping the "peace dividend" by shifting more federal dollars into social programs while reducing the federal deficit.

Boeing CEO Phil Condit sensed a window of opportunity to broaden the business base beyond airliners and restore the eroded portfolio of defense contracts. Starting in 1996, the Boeing Company was reshaped by a series of acquisitions (parts of Rockwell and Hughes) and a merger with the McDonnell-Douglas Corporation.

Lapses in executive judgment and other serious management problems became evident. A chief financial officer (Michael Sears) went to jail for illegal dealings with an Air Force senior procurement official (Darlene Druyun), and two separate CEOs departed under duress (Phil Condit and Harry Stonecipher), while dozens of lesser executives were purged from the ranks. Workplace insecurity reigned as many major operating locations of the newly consolidated company were shut down, divested, or reorganized.

Schedule, supply chain, and technical problems beset the Boeing 787 airliner program. They became a visible and embarrassing public consequence of the internal chaos. The entire 787 flight-test fleet was grounded for a time in late 2010 because of electrical issues. On rare occasions, batteries aboard them burst into flames. For a time, lines of undeliverable 787 aircraft occupied most every bit of available tarmac surrounding the Boeing Everett Factory. Years and billions of dollars were required to get the 787 program onto an even keel.

Two items remained sacrosanct during this turbulent period: the name of the company and quickly returning to the values instilled by William Boeing. These included engineering excellence, manufacturing acumen, financial solvency, and aggressive marketing combined with scrupulous business dealings. The result has been increases to sales, profits, stock valuation, and public esteem.

William Boeing's tenure with the company was a mere 18 years (from mid-1916 to mid-1934), but the values he demanded once again drive the corporation 82 years after his departure.

Boeing operates the largest privately funded fire department in the world, as evidenced by the apparatus on display here in 1991. The Boeing Field fleet (shown) is only one of many Boeing-operated fire stations. Boeing flight operations are routinely conducted out of Seattle's Boeing Field, Renton Airport, and Paine Field at Everett.

The V-22 Osprey is a tilt-rotor military aircraft that has the vertical takeoff and landing capabilities of a helicopter combined with the cruise speed and range of a fixed-wing aircraft. The project was launched in 1983 as a joint venture between Boeing Rotorcraft and Bell Helicopters.

Security officer Dan Carroll waves a driver through the fence line and onto Boeing premises. Flight line security procedures are spelled out; however, they were updated and tightened after the hijacks and attacks of September 11, 2001. Specially trained K-9 dog units now patrol some Boeing sites. Protecting the proprietary data stored in Boeing computers is a less visible but equally important task in a world rife with electronic snooping.

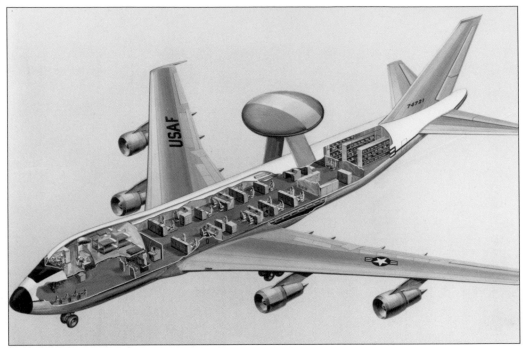

This artist's rendering shows AWACS (Aircraft Warning and Control System) installed in a 747 airframe—which never happened. The 707 remained in low-rate production beyond its commercial life as a military platform. Eventually, four AWACS airplanes were delivered to Japan in Model 767 airframes because the Model 707 production line was finally shut down in 1979 after a 21-year run.

The following news item was reported in February 1972: "The first AWACS plane makes its maiden flight. This is one of two 707-320Bs modified to include advanced radar, data processing, navigation, and communications equipment."

The E-3A Sentry sports a rotating radar dome that is 6 feet thick and 30 feet in diameter. Sophisticated Doppler radar and onboard computers give AWACS crews the ability to control air battles from a safe distance. Midair refueling enables missions of 24 hours. With a crew of 40 (including students), lavatory capacity can become an operating constraint.

The first military role for the Model 737 was navigator trainer designated T-43 Gator. An order for 19 planes was placed in 1971, and this contract helped keep the faltering production line open during that difficult time. The 737 has since performed many other military roles, including the most recent P-8 Poseidon for the US Navy.

A technology called "un-ducted fan" evolved in the 1980s, and an airplane (the 7J7) was conceived to utilize it. The following news item was reported in 1987: "The 7J7 does not attract orders from airlines, and so, it is scrapped and design efforts are redirected."

Several diversification initiatives (e.g., streetcars, people movers, and computing services) were undertaken in the wake of the 1970 airliner market collapse. One of them was large turbine-powered boats (separate versions for commercial passenger and military use) that rode above the water on submerged foils, which generated lift like wings on an airplane. None of the diversification attempts was a great success, however.

Balloons drift into the sky at Renton in celebration of the 5,000th Model 737 that was readied for delivery to Southwest Airlines on February 14, 2006. The sawtooth roof and ramps into Lake Washington are evidence of the plant's seaplane production during World War II. Aircraft built at this site include B-29, C/KC-97, every KC-135, 707, 727, and 757. The plant is now solely devoted to 737 assembly, with an anticipated rate of 52 per month.

Lockheed Martin was the prime contractor on the F-22 Raptor, believed to be the most formidable fighter aircraft in the world. Boeing performed assembly of the aft body, integrated software, and provided training. In 2009, production was prematurely halted at 187 operational jets because the funding was needed for war in Iraq.

Like the first 737 (now in a museum after retirement from NASA) and the first 767 (which went into an experimental Army project), the first 757 found a home as a flying test bed for the F-22 program. As this model shows, the nose of an F-22 was spliced onto the front, while wings were attached above the cockpit. F-22 flight control software could then be validated (and even updated) during airborne testing.

Model 767-2C first took to the sky at Paine Field on the rain-dampened morning of December 28, 2014. The airplane, designated KC-46 Pegasus by the Air Force, taxied into takeoff position and held there briefly pending the imminent arrival of two inbound T-33 chase planes from Boeing Field. After a leisurely 360-degree turn to the left, the chase planes immediately rendezvoused with their target as the three-ship formation climbed out of sight. The KC-46 will keep the 767 production line open for years to come. (Both, photograph by Carl Fredrickson.)

X-32B STOVL
Concept Demonstrator

The Boeing entry into the Joint Strike Fighter (JSF) competition was the X-32. Like the YC-14, it was another homely but innovative design that failed to win a production contract. Lockheed Martin won the fly-off with the F-35 Lightning II, but cost, schedule, and performance issues have plagued the early years of the JSF program.

As Lockheed departed the airliner business and Douglas began to flounder after the mid-1970s, a formidable new competitor emerged. Airbus is a consortium underwritten by some of the wealthiest European countries. Final assembly is performed in Toulouse, France, and there is a perennial battle between Airbus and Boeing over world market share.

A fleet of four heavily modified 747-400s was created to move 787 assemblies around the world. Airplane parts are light but bulky. The tail of this Dreamlifter swings open to load and unload the parts. The main cargo compartment is not pressurized. An airline holds the contract to operate these specialized airplanes.

Eight

WELCOME TO CHARLESTON

As the new millennium approached, senior Boeing executives began to grow frustrated with their traditional home in western Washington.

Local governments were sometimes uncooperative or greedy for more tax revenue. Occasional strikes caused production to halt, profits to plummet, and customers to fume as delivery dates for needed airliners were missed. Furthermore, ever-increasing regional traffic congestion made it difficult to move parts between plants, and employees suffered as commute times mounted. These factors contributed to a decision to seek other operating venues.

Boeing first relocated its corporate headquarters from Seattle to Chicago in September 2001, while pondering the merits of other locations for new or expanded operations. Development of a revolutionary new airliner was announced in 2003. Built of composite rather than aluminum, it could fly ultralong distances, with better fuel economy than any of its competitors. Electric systems would replace the traditional hydraulics, and "bleed air" technology would be used for engine start, cabin pressurization, braking, and movement of the control surfaces.

The airplane would be built in large assemblies by various worldwide risk-sharing partners. Vought Aircraft Industries created a new factory at the Charleston International Airport in South Carolina to fabricate a large piece of the aft fuselage. In a separate (but adjacent) building, Global Aeronautica (a joint venture between Vought and Alenia of Italy) would then install the wiring and other components. A bumpy start-up was experienced. Serious schedule and production woes soon engulfed the 787 program. Some deliveries were to run three years behind schedule.

Taking drastic action, Boeing intervened and took over both operations in 2009. Despite the technical challenges, Boeing executives were elated with the cooperative stance of government and labor. Decertification of the only on-site union contributed to a decision to significantly expand the operation. Construction of a 787 final-assembly building commenced. It dwarfed the original two buildings and would augment Everett 787 assembly. The crown jewel of Boeing South Carolina is a world-class Delivery Center where airline customers from around the world come to accept delivery of 787 aircraft.

This aerial view shows the Boeing Charleston site. Room for expansion is constrained because the airport hosts Charleston Air Force Base (with a bustling fleet of C-17 Globemaster III airlifters), the civilian airline terminal (partially visible at upper right), and the newly constructed Boeing plant. Visible are the three main factory buildings, the flight line, and employee parking. The Delivery

Center is at center right. The taxiway at upper right enables test flights, delivery departures, and frequent Dreamlifter operations. Air-conditioning keeps the indoor workspaces comfortable even during the hot South Carolina summers.

The 787 final-assembly building is shown under construction. North Charleston will be the world's sole source of the largest version of the Model 787 aircraft (dubbed the 787-10) because the fuselage is too long to fit aboard the Dreamlifter. The 787 is the only Boeing product simultaneously produced at two sites: Everett and Charleston.

The 787 is the first airliner to be fabricated primarily from composite, which is stronger than metal, resists corrosion, and is expected to last longer. Cabin pressurization can be increased because of the greater strength. Passengers benefit on long flights because dehydration and the bad effects of higher cabin altitudes are reduced.

At press time, the president of Boeing Commercial Airplanes is Raymond L. Conner (center), seen here touring the Charleston plant while on a visit. Conner joined the Boeing Company in 1977 as a mechanic working on the Model 727 assembly line, earned an advanced education as a working adult, and has subsequently held a variety of executive positions.

Body sections of Boeing aircraft have been consistently numbered for many decades. The aft fuselage is dubbed Section 47. The 787 fuselage is fabricated from large composite pieces that are baked in huge industrial ovens called autoclaves. Section 46 will be attached to Section 47 and then either flown to Everett or towed to the adjacent final-assembly building.

DISCOVER THOUSANDS OF LOCAL HISTORY BOOKS FEATURING MILLIONS OF VINTAGE IMAGES

Arcadia Publishing, the leading local history publisher in the United States, is committed to making history accessible and meaningful through publishing books that celebrate and preserve the heritage of America's people and places.

Find more books like this at
www.arcadiapublishing.com

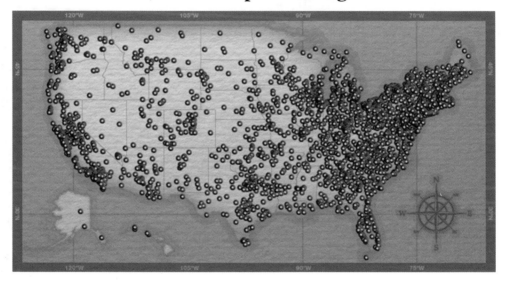

Search for your hometown history, your old stomping grounds, and even your favorite sports team.